A+
books

A Day in the Life of a
CHEETAH
A 4D BOOK

by Lisa J. Amstutz

**Consultant: Robert T. Mason
Professor of Integrative Biology
J.C. Braly Curator of Vertebrates
Oregon State University**

PEBBLE
a capstone imprint

Download the Capstone 4D app!

- Ask an adult to download the Capstone 4D app.
- Scan the cover and stars inside the book for additional content.

When you scan a spread, you'll find
fun extra stuff to go with this book!
You can also find these things
on the web at www.capstone4D.com
using the password: cheetah.31718

A+ Books are published by Pebble
1710 Roe Crest Drive, North Mankato, Minnesota 56003
www.mycapstone.com

Library of Congress Cataloging-in-Publication Data
Names: Amstutz, Lisa J., author.
Title: A day in the life of a cheetah : a 4D book / by Lisa J. Amstutz.
Description: North Mankato, Minnesota : an imprint of Pebble, [2019] |
  Series: A+ books. A day in the life | Audience: Age 4–8.
Identifiers: LCCN 2018006119 (print) | LCCN 2018009140 (ebook) |
  ISBN 9781543531732 (eBook PDF) | ISBN 9781543531718 (library binding) |
  ISBN 9781543531725 (paperback)
Subjects: LCSH: Cheetah—Life cycles—Juvenile literature.
Classification: LCC QL737.C23 (ebook) | LCC QL737.C23 A4657 2019 (print) |
  DDC 599.75/9156—dc23
LC record available at https://lccn.loc.gov/2018006119

Editorial Credits
Gina Kammer, editor; Jennifer Bergstrom, designer;
Morgan Walters, media researcher; Laura Manthe, production specialist

Photo Credits
Newscom: Suzi Eszterhas/ Minden Pictures, 6, 7; Shutterstock: 2630ben, 11, Alexey Osokin, 15,
AndreAnita, Cover, Antero Topp, 12, C_Schmittmann, 18, Chris Fourie, 14, Corrie Barnard, 8, Daniel
Rechsteiner, 19, Dr Ajay Kumar Singh, 20, 29, Gary Cox, 23, gualtiero boffi, 21, GUDKOV ANDREY,
25, Hussain Nalwala, 9, Ihnatovich Maryia, Cover, design element, JaySi, 4, Maggy Meyer, 17,
Mark Bridger, 1, Paul Reeves Photography, 26, Sharon Haeger, 5, 30, sitayi, 27, Stuart G Porter, 24,
Utopia_88, 22, wimpi, 13

Note to Parents, Teachers, and Librarians

This book uses full color photographs and a nonfiction format to introduce the concept of a
cheetah's day. *A Day in the Life of a Cheetah* is designed to be read aloud to a pre-reader or to be read
independently by an early reader. Photographs help listeners and early readers understand the text
and concepts discussed. The book encourages further learning by including the following sections:
Table of Contents, Glossary, Read More, Internet Sites, Critical Thinking Questions, and Index. Early
readers may need assistance using these features.

TABLE OF CONTENTS

A Cheetah's Day

As the sun rises over the dry grass, a cheetah lifts her head. She looks around. Like most cheetahs, she lives on the African savanna. A few cheetahs live in Asia as well.

HUNGRY!

Five cubs wake and stretch. They are hungry. The cheetah lies on her side while the cubs nurse. Soon their bellies are full of warm milk. They pounce and play.

Each cub has a line of fluffy hair on its back. It is called a mantle. It may help hide the cub in the tall grass. As the cub grows, the mantle turns into a small mane.

The cheetah is hungry too. *CHURR!* She calls to her cubs. She nudges them to a hiding spot. Then she heads out to hunt.

CHURR!

SNIFF, SNIFF. The cheetah smells food. She follows her nose. There! She spots an antelope. Crouching low, she sneaks closer. Her tan fur and spots blend in with the grass. They make it hard for her prey to see her. Her prey is the animal she hunts.

The cheetah has about 2,000 spots. They are different from any other cheetah's. She also has streaks on her face that look like tears.

WHOOSH! The cheetah is off. Her prey zigzags as it runs. But the cheetah is fast. The cheetah's long legs take giant leaps. With each step, she covers about 23 feet (7 meters).

WHOOSH!

Her long tail helps her steer. She reaches a speed of nearly 70 miles (113 kilometers) per hour. That is as fast as a car on a highway!

With one last leap, the cheetah reaches out. She hooks the antelope's leg with her large, sharp dewclaw. The animal trips and falls.

Dewclaw

HOOK!

The cheetah bites its throat. She holds the animal until it stops moving. Then she drags the body to the shade. She lies down, panting. She must cool her body before eating.

The cheetah tears into her meal. She can eat up to 20 pounds (9 kilograms) of meat in less than two hours. Gazelle and antelope are her main foods. She also eats rabbits, birds, and other small animals.

The cheetah eats until her belly is full. Now she must find her cubs. *CHURR! CHURR!* she calls. She hears a soft reply. She trots off to find them. The cubs are happy to see their mother. They are hungry again.

The cubs eat. When they are full, they purr. Now it is time for a nap. They find some shade.

PURR!

Just then, the cheetah sniffs the air.
Uh-oh! Danger! A hyena is nearby.

A hyena is too small to kill an adult cheetah. But it would eat a cub. Hyenas and lions kill many young cheetahs. Lions kill adult cheetahs too.

The cheetah ducks down to watch. She is not a good fighter. But she is ready to defend her cubs.

READY!

Luckily, the hyena moves on.
It will look for easier prey.
The family is safe for now.

The mother licks her cubs to clean them. Her tongue is covered with tiny hooks. It acts like a comb.

She gives herself a bath too. She licks the parts she can reach. Then she licks her paws and grooms her head.

LICK!

The sky turns pink and fades to black. The cheetah pulls her cubs near. She closes her eyes and waits for morning.

Good night, cheetah!

LIFE CYCLE OF A
CHEETAH

1

When she is around **TWO YEARS OLD,** a female cheetah finds a mate.

2

The female carries her babies inside her body for **90** to **98** **DAYS.**

3

Then the cheetah gives birth to a litter of **3** to **6 CUBS.** They drink milk from their mother.

4

At about **6** to **8 WEEKS** of age, the young begin to eat meat. By **4** to **5 MONTHS,** they are weaned.

5

When they are **12** to **20 MONTHS** old, the cubs are ready to live on their own.

Glossary

defend—to try to keep someone or something from being changed or harmed

dewclaw—a sharp claw that is behind and higher than an animal's other claws

groom—to clean and make an animal look neat

mane—long, thick hair that grows on the head and neck of some animals

mantle—thick, fluffy fur on a cub's back that is thought to help hide it in the grass

mate—the male or female partner of a pair of animals

nurse—to drink mother's milk

prey—an animal hunted by another animal for food

savanna—a flat, grassy area of land with few or no trees

weaned—the point at which young mammals are ready to eat food rather than drink their mother's milk

Read More

Archer, Claire. *Cheetahs.* Big Cats. Minneapolis: Abdo Kids, 2014.

Spilsbury, Louise. *Save the Cheetah.* Animal SOS! New York: Windmill Books, 2014.

Statts, Leo. *Cheetahs.* Zoom in on Savanna Animals. Minneapolis: Abdo Zoom, 2017.

Internet Sites

Use FactHound to find Internet sites related to this book.

Visit *www.facthound.com*

Just type in 9781543531718 and go.

 **Super-cool stuff!** Check out projects, games and lots more at **www.capstonekids.com**

★ Critical Thinking Questions

1. Name three foods that are part of a cheetah's diet.

2. Page 7 says that cheetah cubs have a mantle. Use the glossary on page 31 to define *mantle*.

3. How does a cheetah take a bath?

4. How does a cheetah hunt?

Index